With WK in the Workshop

Works by Brian Dedora:

With WK in the Workshop: A Memoir of William Kurelek
(Aya Press/The Mercury Press, 1989)
White Light (Aya Press, 1987)
The Dream
He Moved
What a City Was
A Posteriori
The Circle
July 21, 1979
The Limited Edition
Archeo-Linguistics: ONLY A STONE'S THROW,
by Adrian Fortesque
Frames
Some Thoughts on the Turning of the Year 81-82
A B.C. Childhood, with bpNichol
"HAND"
A Table of Contents
The Mouse

With WK in the Workshop

A MEMOIR OF WILLIAM KURELEK

Brian Dedora

INTRODUCTION BY RAMSAY COOK

With Paintings, Drawings, and Photographs
by William Kurelek

Aya Press / The Mercury Press
Stratford, Ontario

ACKNOWLEDGEMENTS:
I would like to thank Rachel Atlas, who taped our conversations about Kurelek and typed
them out for me, Martha Hutner Black, with whom I had detailed talks concerning the
Tool Paintings, and Bev Daurio who said yes. *Brian Dedora*

Aya Press/The Mercury Press gratefully acknowledges the financial assistance of the
Canada Council and the Ontario Arts Council.

Quotes from: *O Toronto*, William Kurelek, New Press, Toronto, 1973;
Someone with Me: An Autobiography of William Kurelek, William Kurelek,
McClelland and Stewart, Toronto, 1980.

Cover design and production co-ordination: The Blue Pencil
Typeset at The Beacon Herald, Stratford, Ontario
Printed and bound in Canada by Hignell Printing Ltd.
Photography of paintings and drawings: Tom Moore

The publishers are grateful to Mr. Av Isaacs and The Isaacs Gallery, for their co-operation
and support, and for their gracious assistance beyond reasonable expectation; to Martha
Black, for her help and good guidance; to Ramsay Cook; to Jean Kurelek; and especially
to B.D., who never really went away.

U of T.   995 – 878   2/91

Canadian Cataloguing in Publication

Dedora, Brian, 1946—
   With WK in the workshop

ISBN 0-920544-68-1

1. Kurelek, William, 1927-1977. 2. Painters —
Canada — Biography. 3. Dedora, Brian, 1946-
I. Kurelek, William, 1927-1977. II. Title.

ND249.K87D4 1989   759.11   C89-094630-2

Aya Press / The Mercury Press
Box 1153, Station F   Box 446
Toronto, Ontario   Stratford, Ontario
Canada M4Y 2T8   Canada N5A 6T3

Contents

INTRODUCTION

REMEMBRANCE OF THINGS PAST

> "And suddenly the memory revealed itself."
> — *Marcel Proust*

Av Isaacs' gallery, first in Toronto's "Greenwich Village," and later on Yonge Street, was so central to the flowering of the avant garde in the 1960s that it is easy to forget that an extraordinary painter of the school of Bosch and Breughel also found a home there. William Kurelek was that painter, one of the great Christian artists of this century, a craftsman of unusual skill, both on canvas and in the framing shop. His imagination constantly reshaped his memories, memories of his Ukrainian heritage, his prairie childhood and youth, and his intense religious convictions, into startlingly original paintings. In The Isaacs Gallery, where Kurelek first showed his work, and where he earned his living as a picture framer, he blossomed into a painter of distinction.

William Kurelek's youth and early manhood were times of deep trouble, filled with doubts, fears, and hostilities, demons that eventually sent him to find psychiatric help. He recalled those excruciating years in his astonishingly candid autobiography, *Someone with Me*. Psychiatry, conversion to Catholicism, and his wife Jean, gradually restored Kurelek to the life he wanted, the life of an artist. But credit should also be given to the framing shop at The Isaacs Gallery. There, for over a decade, Kurelek did the work and found the friends that made painting and supporting a growing family possible. There with Stan Beecham and Brian Dedora, and sometimes others, Kurelek practised the framer's craft that he had learned during his years in England. Over this brood of men, practising and learning a craft that required both imagination and skill, presided Av Isaacs, learning his new trade as an art dealer.

Kurelek and Isaacs were an odd couple — at least on the superficial view. Isaacs, who had grown up in Winnipeg and studied political science at the University of Toronto, was a free-spirited, secular Jew with an eye and an ear for the new in art and jazz. Kurelek came from a Ukrainian immigrant, farm background. Neither university nor art school appealed to him much, and after his conversion to Catholicism, he held and expressed his religious convictions with passionate determination. For him the modern, secular world held only danger, and his view of it verged on the apocalyptic. Sometimes Kurelek and Isaacs quarrelled, for in his dark moods Kurelek was stubborn and suspicious — and naive. He was often offended by what he thought of as the "pornographic" pictures that were sometimes shown in the Gallery. But Isaacs had quickly learned how to work with difficult artists — Kurelek was far from the only one in the Isaacs' circle — and he recognized that Kurelek's temperament was all of a piece: the painter, the believer, the man of moods, all went together. And Kurelek knew that he had found in Av Isaacs much more than a dealer; he had found a friend, someone who accepted him as he was and believed in his work.

Isaacs gave Kurelek his first chance in Toronto: he could show his paintings of "farm scenes," boyhood memories, immigrant life, and, as often as possible, works filled with Christian allegories and moral admonition. There in the midst of the tumbling, tumbleweed on the prairie would appear Christ crucified on a fence post or, under the full moon shining on a peaceful house, a speeding Hound of Heaven. Kurelek thought of himself as an evangelist called to use his artistic talent as a witness to his Christian beliefs. Sometimes he would paint what he disparagingly dubbed "pot-boilers," paintings of seeming innocence and nostalgia. But even in these works a little cross would be slipped in somewhere, often in his signature. Gradually, Kurelek became a known and sought-after painter, though his critics were frequently puzzled by the conflicts of good and evil, of demons gnawing on the icons of secularism, that so often stood almost brutally in the foreground of his canvases.

Here was surely an improbable member of the Isaacs' ensemble? Where did he fit in with the likes of William Ronald, Dennis Burton, Gordon Rayner, Graham Coughtry, Joyce Wieland, Robert Markle and Michael Snow — the avant garde? In a sense, Kurelek didn't fit — there, or anywhere. He was in, but not of, the modern art scene in Toronto. Yet, in another way, he fitted well enough, though not with the Bohemian life-style or the artistic goals of the Isaacs' crowd. He belonged because he, too, had set himself against the conventional stream of picture-making. He had his own vision of what art should be and was willing, if necessary, to remain an outsider if that was what making his kind of art demanded. Like his Ukrainian forebears, he would persist, he would make do.

Of course, he could always fall back on the workshop. And not only to make a living. It is only with Brian Dedora's intimate account of the framing shop that we are let into that underground of Stan, and Brian and Bill — and Av. Here we meet Kurelek the craftsman, the joker, the teacher. For a man who found close companionship difficult at best, the workshop became a place almost as important to the stability of his daily life as the bog on his father's farm was to his imaginative life. The workshop provided Kurelek with another home and family, complete with the warmth, the friction and the laughter which make family life. Or perhaps better, it was a brotherhood where the rites, rituals and bonds were unspoken but ever-present. Brian Dedora's evocation of this brotherhood has such poignancy, re-creating the mood and spirit of that place with emotional intensity, that a new understanding of William Kurelek emerges. Like Kurelek, Dedora has translated memory into art.

Reading Dedora's memoir, I, too, remembered things past, and realized what I owed to William Kurelek. In the early 1960s, as I was awakening to the emotions that paint on canvas stirred in me, I began, rather timidly, to visit the galleries around Toronto. It was then that I first discovered the work of William Kurelek and The Isaacs Gallery. As a prairie boy, I was naturally drawn to the images of rural life in Western Canada, especially those that combined Christian symbolism and moral outrage with the anecdotes of daily life. These pictures seemed to sum up for me what growing up during the Depression on the prairies had meant — childhood memory mixed with adult understanding. One Saturday I dropped into The Isaacs Gallery and found myself in the midst of a noisy, well-dressed show-opening crowd. Knowing no-one, I was able to look, uninterrupted, at a series of works depicting one of Kurelek's essential themes: the story of Ukrainian settlement on the prairies. Before leaving, I glanced around the gallery. There, in a corner, stood an uneasy-looking, stocky man, his hair cut unfashionably short for the long-haired sixties, wearing an orange shirt, carefully embroidered in the traditional Ukrainian fashion. He was alone — not in the universe, or even in the world. But still, alone.

That memory of William Kurelek has always stayed with me. It came into sharp focus again as I read Brian Dedora's gentle, powerful memoir.

RAMSAY COOK

*These photographs, the only photos
of the Workshop,
were shot by William Kurelek
and given to the author.*

*The gift of these negatives
became the incentive to write this book.*

Brian Dedora

The screech of nails being withdrawn from dry wood echoed against the bare walls. Wood clawed with hammers and smashed with crowbars lay in heaps, ready to be discarded. Sawdust, settled for years in unswept corners and crannies, swarmed and stung the eyes. Work benches, torn apart and scattered, turned up in recognizable bits and pieces: Stan's plywood chisel holder; Bill's gessoed counter top; my set of bunks for holding glass — heaped and ruined.

When the workmen started hauling the piles out to the garbage truck a kid came up the alley. He began taking bits of moulding out of the truck and piling them to one side. When the decision to close the shop was made, we sent out flyers to all the art schools to sell off the mouldings and matboards cheap — no response. I asked the kid what he thought he was doing.

"Taking your garbage."

"Well, if nobody else wants it you're not going to get it. Get lost."

Coughtry said he couldn't believe it: the Isaacs Gallery without a workshop. Av without a workshop. He just couldn't believe it. Neither could I.

One

THE WORKSHOP

I am broke and working part time for twenty-two dollars a week. I hear the Isaacs need a fitter. I walk in on Saturday and see Mr. Isaacs. He asks me what experience I have; I tell him the only thing I have been doing is fitting. Actually, I've been working as a pancake fitter for shops that order everything from a wholesaler by number code. When the order comes in with frame, mat, glass and backing, you clean the glass, tape the artwork, and pancake it together. Pancake, pancake. Wham, bam, thank you, ma'am. I tell him I am really fast. He hires me on the spot to report to Stan Beecham at nine on Monday morning. Two weeks before Christmas, they are working on orders dated from October.

Sunday night storms freezing rain. Tree branches crack in the wind outside the kitchen window. The kitchen is dark. I wait for the rumble of the streetcar and run out, cold.

Outside the workshop in the alley, I wait, peer inside at the light. The men moving around. The Isaacs Gallery. A real job.

I push in the door, slide past a pile of crates spewing shredded newspaper into a main aisleway leading down the centre of the shop. I am motioned forward by one of the men to another room to meet Stan Beecham. He takes me into another room to meet Hal. I am to work with Hal as a second fitter.

Later in the morning, a man from the first room comes down to our end, and asks me if I am Ukrainian. Nobody has ever asked me that question. As a matter of fact, I am. He puts out his hand and says, so am I, I guess that makes us brothers. I'm Bill Kurelek.

13

Two

A circle divided into quarters: around this circuit, work proceeds with its division of labour and craft.

Frame and mat samples chosen in the gallery are written up on work orders. Customers' artwork is numbered according to this order. Stan picks up the orders and the artwork, and brings them next door, into the workshop.

Stan clips the orders to a clipboard on the mitre saw, places the artwork in the fitter's room in bunks. Work then proceeds from Stan, who cuts and joins the desired frames and mats. He passes the frame to the finisher, and the mats to the fitter. Both mat and frame have the work order number scribbled on the back.

The finisher takes the raw frame, noting the desired finish on the work order, and proceeds to apply that finish. He makes gesso for gold or silver leaf, lays imitation leaf on moulding lengths to be kept in stock for quick cutting and assembly, sprays lacquer finishes, gilds and burnishes, and, if desired, antiques the finish. When the frame is finished and dry, the finisher takes the frame to the fitter.

The fitter, on receiving the work order and the frame, matches it with the mats ordered and the artwork. He cuts glass and backboard, cleans and polishes the glass, lays down the mat with the artwork and backing, then fits the whole into the frame and nails it into place. He papers the back and wires the frame according to weight. He also assembles aluminum frames and handwraps liners and mats with silk, linen and velvet. He wraps the completed frame in brown paper and writes the name of the customer on it, and takes the package and work order back to the gallery.

I arrive broke, depressed and lacking in confidence. It is the shop environment and work that pull me out of the grip of past feelings and pressures into the present, wounded self-image healed by the acquisition of skills and hard work. Bill has rebuilt his life in the same way.

Smoothing down gessoed frames, preparing the grounds on which the gold is laid, burnishing the gold; the process so integrated it is only in the burnishing you discover if the grounds are properly laid. Allusions to our groundwork: Bill's artistic struggle, my struggle to write. His quiet support. We didn't always talk, but when we did, he was astute and sensitive.

15

Three

Pine, oak, mahogany, walnut and basswood. Table saw. Mitre saw. Chisels: firmer, and bevelled. Gouges. Moulding planes, jack, block, and rebate planes. Screws, nails, white glue, scotch glue, wood rasps and files: half round and rat tail. Knife blades and whetstone. Panel saw and dovetail saw. Crosscut and plywood blades. Dado blades. Measuring tapes, jaw vise, hammer; c-clamps, spring clamps, bar clamps; shooting board, scrapers, veneer hammer, drills and twist bits. Shell bits, countersinks and forstners. Try square, marking gauge, spokeshave, punches and awls. Gesso, clay, aniline stains, methyl hydrate, lacquer and lacquer reducer. Shellac, shellac sticks, graphite, sandpaper 120 and 220. Rubbers, fixative, raw umber, yellow ochre, tempera powders, black ink, brushes, steel wool, rabbitskin glue, wax, gold size, genuine gold and silver leaf. Metal leaf, agates, tips, linseed oil, turps, natural sponge, chalk, water, latex, spatula, gesso combs, rottenstone and pumice. Cardboard, duplex board, kraft paper, finishing nails, sidecutters, paper trimmers, glass cutter, pliers, awl, steam iron, razor blades and knives. Picture wire, screw-eyes, turnbuckles, spring fasteners, allen keys, stapler, needlenose, linen tape, gum tape, masking tape, scotch tape, scissors, bone folder, white glue, rollers, linens, silks and velvets. Flat and round head, slot and robertson, one and two holed hangers, glass, mats and matboards.

Those are the nouns we handled.

These are the verbs we performed:

Mitring, lapping, butting, bevelling, chamfering, gouging, chiselling, sawing, planing, rasping, filing, sharpening, shaping, scraping, measuring, fly flecking, cowlicking, smudging, hand dragging, polishing, laying, burnishing, sanding, wiping, sponging, waxing, cutting, folding, hinging, mounting, papering, wiring, cutting and joining, finishing and fitting.

I didn't know a quarter of this vocabulary before I arrived.

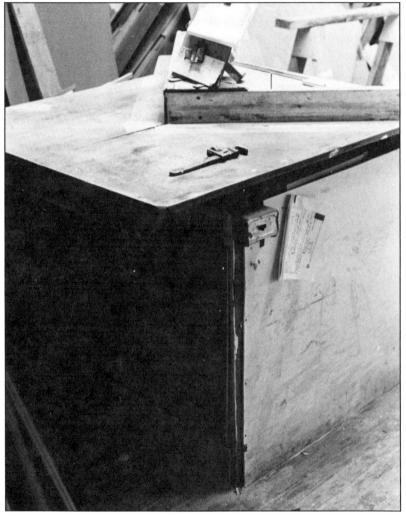

Four

My relationship with Bill grows and is established in the early mornings. On coming to the shop early I catch Bill after his night's work. He keeps a bedroll which he lays out on one of the work benches to grab a nap.

The procedure for laying gold leaf is precarious. The gilder fits a cushioned leather palette over his left hand and thumbtacks a book of gold leaf to the left side. Lifting the pages of the book with his gilder's knife, he lays the knife over the leaf and gently blows the leaf over the blade. He picks up the leaf and transfers it to the right side of the cushion and blows the leaf back over the blade and flat out on the cushion. He then cuts the leaf to the width required for the moulding. When the leaf is cut, he drops his knife. In his left hand he holds the gilder's tip. He takes the tip in his right hand, touches it to his hair for the oil, or if his hair is dry, to his cheek, previously covered in oil. He then touches the tip (being as wide as a leaf of gold) to the leaf along its edge and picks up the leaf. The leaf, being a few thousandths of an inch thick, wavers in any breeze. Again he transfers the tip with the leaf to his left hand. The right hand now free paints the frame with gilding liqueur, a mixture of rabbitskin glue, water and alcohol. While the frame is wet, the tip with the leaf is transferred back to the right hand and held over the frame. The free edge is touched to the liqueur. As the chalk in the gesso is thirsty, it draws the water to itself and pulls the leaf to its shape as you move the tip quickly over the contour of the frame. This is repeated until the entire frame is covered.

One morning, Bill asks me if I've brought him an apple. I joke, I ate it on the way to work. Curiosity gets the better of me, and I ask why. Bill replies, all students bring their teachers an apple. He is going to teach me how to gild.

Watching Bill lay gold, the frame on his bench smooth and ready. Bill picks up leaf from his gilder's pad, the wide tip brushes his hair, the leaf thin and waving. He almost thwacks the gold in place: thwack, thwack, thwack. The gold in the light rippling, swooning into place, forming itself to the contours of the frame to catch light and hold shade, the glow of it in our faces: Bill excited, me in awe.

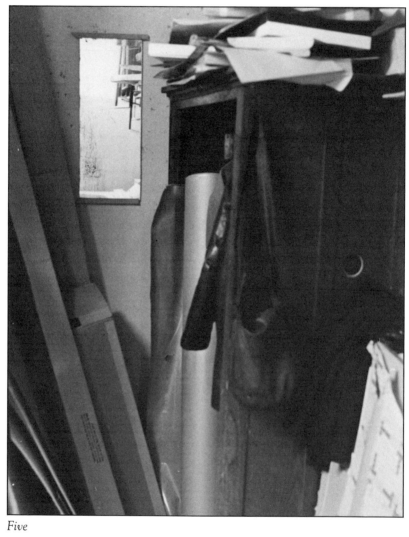

Five

I listen to Stan prepare a frame for the Lieutenant Governor of Ontario. The frame is to be wider than any moulding we carry. It has to be cut and shaped by hand. Using only a table saw and a jack plane, Stan rounds and shapes the moulding from undressed pine. Throughout the shop you could hear the sound of the plane whining down the length of wood in one long even stroke, an unbroken sound ending in the swish of shavings falling to the floor. The planing continued for hours until the frame was perfectly matched and shaped from four separate pieces of wood.

Stan tells me to curb my swearing; if it's going that badly, do something else.

Stan wears a tie to work. A British trained craftsman taught to follow a set of plans. He does, assiduously.

He teaches me the names and uses of tools, describes making furniture: walnut cabinets, serpentine desks. From one of his trips, he brings me a present of books on woodworking and period furniture design.

Stan, the true and trained craftsman — to follow and do, to execute with skill this or that task — was misunderstood in a Toronto that was raw, its demands for craftsmanship superficial, working for Eaton's restoring scratched reproduction furniture. He tells me this, tells me about work in England, foot pedaled fret saws, the making of dovetails, the elimination of bloom in a French polish with a sheet of flame that drives out moisture without scorching. Skills not lost, but in Toronto, unrequested.

Arriving in the early morning through the rain along Yorkville and down the laneway, the concrete brown with wet. The back door: the lights are on, Bill is there. The yellow light shining in the morning gray through the door. Into the warmth, the white of the gessoed benches and walls, smells of wood, shellac and glue.

Through the windows at the end of the shop on a late afternoon when the snow first falls, there is a light that reflects back softly. Inside, the shop hums; outside, white silence.

The windows at the end of the shop on a day in late April when it rains. The gray lights the boxes, the packing crates, the lengths of lumber.

Through the windows at the back of the shop you can see the drooping lilacs where the sun streams in, where sawdust swirls.

At the back of the shop the doors are thrown open. It's summer. Hollyhocks tower over the neighbour's sway-back fence.

Through the windows at the back you can watch the days grow shorter, see the odd wind-blown leaf, feel the draught under the door.

On November 11 at 11 o'clock Stan hangs his head, his work-splayed hands curl on his bench. He is quiet most of the day.

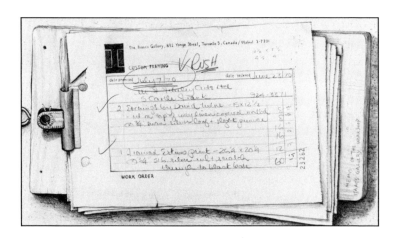

KURELEK

The Toronto Star, *Today Magazine*, November 21, 1981

THE LAST PAINTINGS OF WILLIAM KURELEK *see page 18*

THE KURELEK LEGACY

In the last months of his tortured
life, William Kurelek painted
some of his most serene paintings...

It is often forgotten that Kurelek went through analysis and shock
treatment to come out the other side, his nightmares painted out
for the world to see, shifting to the nightmares in daily life, the shift
to the brighter farm paintings. To talk about his whole life as tortured
or to measure his whole work by the beginning is the stuff of legend
and myth and misinformation of the man working in the frame shop,
the man.

Kurelek first took up framing while undergoing therapy in London.
Having trouble with his eyesight, and worried he could never be
an artist, he turned to framing. He found work framing for Pollacks
in Blue Ball Yard where he first met Stan Beecham. Stan, later, in
Toronto, was hired, and the two formed the core of the Isaacs shop.

Back in Toronto and hoping to work in framing, Bill took frame
samples (around his own work) to the Isaacs Gallery and asked if
there might be work gilding. If Av could interest people in them,
he would take Bill on. Av was interested in the gilded frames, but
excited by the art. Their relationship had begun. The bargain was
struck by Bill; he would work in the shop for ten years. If after that
his paintings were selling he would devote himself to his art.

Six

LONDON, ENGLAND

In Kurelek's autobiography, *Someone with Me*, Kurelek says:

At the time I actually entered the Church I'd already been working for three months for a picture framer. I'd approached some half dozen shops before I chanced on Pollacks. Someone had recommended them to me. The workshop's location goes by the quaint name of "Blue Ball Yard." It is just off St. James Street which is near Green Park and in front of Buckingham Palace. I'd decided to go into picture framing for a living as (a) it was evident I couldn't paint full time because of my eye trouble and (b) I wanted to go into a business that my father might later join me in and (c) it would be my bread and butter profession because it was obvious I couldn't make a living off painting.

...However, before any of these dreams could be realized, I had to learn the picture frame trade myself. And that's how it was that 1957 saw me beginning apprentice work in "Blue Ball Yard."

Mr. and Mrs. Pollack were Czech Jews, refugees from the Nazis, and Mr. Pollack had a first class reputation as frame and antique restorer — perhaps the best in the city. He really had taste and skill. We framed many an Old Master — the real thing, not just reproductions. It was thus a privilege to work for him — but, oh, so hard!

Mr. Pollack was very fat and balding and he worked on a wide table across from me and the foreman, Hans Roeder, a young gilder from Cologne. Completely absorbed in his work he'd hum to himself and be breathing heavily as he gave the final exquisite touches to a frame or an antique. He stayed in his suit so he'd be ready to meet customers in the visiting room if Mrs. Pollack called him. Once in a while he'd peer out over his glasses if something were missing — "Wer hat mein pinzel?" or "Wo ist mein spritzholz?" And then he'd see he'd misplaced it himself. German was the official language in the shop, although not all the employees were German. There was an Indian, Mr. Noolan, who was a deaf mute, and three or more English workers — Stan Beecham, shy Mr. Miller and Stan Westlake. Lillian the mat cutting girl was also English. Finally there was a Chinese boy, Peter, but we never did find out his last name. For a while there we had an Italian, too, but he didn't last long. The deaf mute and the shy girl were the perfect couple for work in the Secret Room which held a jealously harboured trade secret — the artificial cracking of gesso. The rest of us were never allowed to go in there, so that it would remain a trade secret. Down below, in what was once coach stables, was now a big garage stored with hundreds of all kinds of genuine antique carved frames. Mr. Pollack had no use for anything but GENUINE carved frames. And marvel of marvels he remembered every single one of those frames by heart!

I began by stripping some antique chairs and then coating them with gesso. It was tedious work but I fully agreed that where an apprentice should begin is at the bottom. As it was, I was lucky to be taken on as an actual employee. In Germany an apprentice got no pay for the first two years or so. I started at four pounds a week and by the time I left I was drawing eight pounds. At the end of my two years' apprenticeship I was given a little gilding to do. My wages went up whenever I did a specially good job, as for example when I made the harness for a model of a coach and six. My Manitoba farm experience proved invaluable here.

They had hired me on the strength of my trompe l'oeil *paintings for it meant to them that I could do fine, disciplined work. And so whenever there was a painting job I got it. As Pollack was such a perfectionist it was with mixed joy and apprehension that I tackled those special tasks. He knew dead on what colour a thing was to be and not only that, but how to mix that colour, while I never actually learned painting, even in art school. In a way, working at Pollacks was like a continuation of art school. Thus, many of the techniques I learned at Pollacks eventually found their way into my paintings (eg. spattering, and smudging, and sealing, and most important of all gessoing the ground on which my paintings are done).*

Another job I got, especially when the trade was slow, was frame stripping. You use dentist's tools and inch by inch strip a frame down to the original coat of gold which might be several hundred years old. It might take several weeks to do one such frame and if only two inches were done in a day, that was good progress. You had to be ever so careful not to dig in too deep. It was such intense, minute work that I was afraid for my eyes again, but I didn't need to be really. The odd, or perhaps significant fact, is that from the day of my actual reception into the Church till today, sixteen years later, the pain has not returned.

I was also taking evening school then two nights a week; one in picture framing, the other in cabinet work, both at Hammersmith School of Building Arts and Crafts. For a short while I took book illustration as well. The picture frame school was the only one in London, probably in Europe and as Mr. McKay, the red-bearded Scots instructor guessed, "the only one in the world."

One of the cabinet-makers, Stan Beecham, used to have run-ins with the Pollacks too, but he stood up to them in a quiet angry way, something I wasn't able to do. I presented him with some important information about Canada, or so I thought, when he emigrated to there, but my attempt at charity in that direction sort of backfired, for those promotion leaflets turned out to be misleadingly rosy. He stuck it out there, however. Several years later I was back in Canada myself and working for the Isaacs Gallery. Av Isaacs came to me asking about a cabinet-maker of old country vintage. I recommended Stan. So that's how he became my foreman at the Isaacs Gallery workshop. We enjoy once in a while, comparing reminiscences of the "Blue Ball Yard" as if we were veterans of some famous campaign.

Seven

Eight

TORONTO AND THE ISAACS GALLERY

Kurelek goes on to speak about Toronto in *Someone with Me*:

... when I first arrived in Toronto and was going around inquiring about the possibilities of starting a picture framing business, I also here and there inquired about the possibility of exhibiting my paintings. All galleries I tried had politely said, "No, not interested," when I showed them samples of paintings and frames. All that is, except one — Av Isaacs, who then had a shop on Bay and Hayter Streets. He got interested in my paintings mostly. "Could I see you later this year about the possibility of a show of your work?" he wanted to know. I agreed readily enough but couldn't believe he'd remember. He did come to the Reuters to see all my work that fall and mentioned March as an exhibition possibility. Still I refused to raise my hopes. As I said, shortly after my getting down to work on the St. Matthew series the first break came. It was a short-term job of painting Av's gallery. He also said, "I'd give you picture frame work but I've not got it for the giving. However, if you make up some picture frame samples of real gold and silver work at my workshop, I'll see if I can get customers interested."

Thus, at first only a few hours, later a whole day, still later two days a week, I began to work for him. I could now pay my rent. ...There were three men at Av's framing shop in Church and Front Streets, an unused warehouse, and Av kept contact with this shop from his gallery by phone.

Bill brought many things to the shop, in fact he was the spirit of the shop. Kurelek's gilding was of an expertise rooted in an intuitive sense of the materials he was handling. Instead of sanding the gesso coated frame, which gives a very clean edge to the work, he would smooth the gesso with a damp linen rag. What this did was to produce a surface smoothed for gilding, but rounded and showing parts of the moulding that collected more or less gesso than the rest, thus giving the hand finished appearance that it truly was. No slips or slight excess were sanded away. The frame stood not only as handsome object, but flowed around the artwork naturally with no cut corners.

Nine

Kurelek was classically trained as a framer, not only in finishing but in the shapes and contours of classical moulding. Classic moulding was designed in width to take a sheet of gold leaf, full size, halves, thirds, or quarters. These mouldings proceed from the edge of the artwork out: the lip, panel, or flat and cap. This principle of three is contained in nearly all the frames Kurelek made for his own paintings.

Panel design in Kurelek's frames ranges from simple painted panels to panels covered in Ukrainian embroidery, stencils of maple leaves or shamrocks. For a painting of Newfoundland, the panel was pasted with slips of paper on which were printed "Newfie" jokes; the derisory jokes contrast with a beautiful landscape. The frame is extended to comment on the artwork. A prime example in his last series, The Polish Series, is a painting of a cemetery where photos of the gravestones are applied to the panel; no longer just a frame, but a deliberate and conscious attempt to incorporate art and frame.

Frame finishing techniques found their way into Kurelek's paintings. Gesso and gesso modelling become the ground on which he paints. A gesso comb, used to striate wet gesso for effect, gives texture to the fields in his artwork. Spattered ink, used as antiquing in frames, is used for shading, as are smudging techniques. Kurelek often said he was not an artist but a picture maker, a craftsman who could easily employ techniques of one craft to achieve effects in another.

To work side by side, forty hours a week, year after year, requires a sense of humour. Bill's humour was never better than at work. He loved practical jokes. Preparing to sand a raw wood frame, I reached over to pick up my sanding block. It was nailed to the bench. Clawing it off with a hammer, I found neatly written in Bill's hand: APRIL FOOL.

Stan and Bill were constantly involved in contests. Who could write the smallest? Who could cut a one eighth strip of glass from a forty inch cut and break it off in one piece? The wall of predictions was another of their joking contests. On the wall separating the finishing end from the cutting end, predictions were written down and betted on, with stakes ranging from a penny to a nickel. The predictions: no snow by April 11; a green Christmas; apartment building on this site by 1972...

Av had to go to hospital. We all know what happens when the boss is away. The drawing Bill presented to Av showed the mice scampering over the work benches, burning hands in the drymount press and joining dissimilar mouldings.

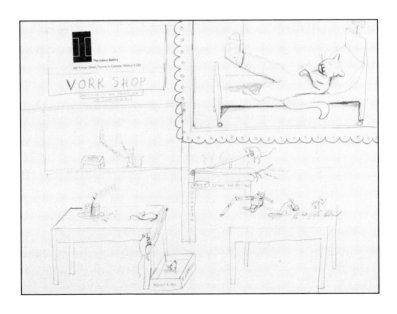

BILL AND I

I saw one of his paintings when I first came to the Isaacs to get work, a painting of a family at breakfast, with spilt milk, tossed-over cornflakes, bacon and eggs, drips and stains, small children, mom and dad. I hated that painting. Underneath the kitchen table, a starving Indian beggar. I was appalled at the naive draftsmanship, both crude and harsh, shocked because of what that beggar was doing. I didn't want to see that rag dressed beggar, his scrawny outstretched hand. As I got to know Kurelek, I realized he would always put that beggar there.

Shortly after I started at the shop, a show of Kurelek's paintings was being sent out. They were assembled in the shop so we could pack and crate them. That's when I first began seeing his paintings: three come to mind.

A still life with a bowl, apples, eggs and a piece of cloth. A standard still life. I was knocked out. The eggs had the grain of their calcium shells; the apples were painted beautifully. They weren't red, they were red with green, with little white spots that you can see on apples, areas where the green and red combine, areas which were green, areas which were red. The bowl, a bowl like my mother used for Christmas pudding, a standard white British crockery bowl. A beautiful painting. I could feel those eggs, feel those apples, I knew the bowl.

There was one of his very early allegorical pieces, a painting divided into three or four different planes. On those planes all sorts of things were happening, psychological things divided up with a huge brick wall, the brick wall like a part of a building, yet not. In subterranean parts, things were going on. I can't remember now all the scenes, but it reminded me of a medieval painting, astounding to see in the 1970s. All those vignettes you could wander through, a story I found easy to read, taken by the dark vision.

Another one was of Kurelek pulling a rickshaw carrying his father, who is whipping him with his tongue, Kurelek pecked at by crows. A horrendous image actually painted and visible. I knew what was going on, I knew exactly what was going on. I couldn't believe a person could paint it for all to see.

Ten

One of the jobs of the fitter was to cut glass. The waste ends were broken into metal garbage pails. I enjoyed it. One day Kurelek said to me, "That's the best part of this job. I used to save them up and break them all at once."

I asked Kurelek about his shock treatment, the idea of which I found abhorrent. "What was it like?" I could hardly envision being strapped down and having all that voltage run through me. "What's it for?" He very matter-of-factly explained that it destroyed brain cells and would destroy memory. If you didn't have those memories you could get on with your life. Science would just obliterate the memory. Kurelek paused for a minute, looked at me, and said, "But the memories are coming back."

In a painting which shows the back view of his head in cross-section, "The Maze," the viewer sees the chambers inside his mind, crammed with bits of paper, notes of paper, all past things, troublesome things, bits of paper settled in his mind. In one of the prairie paintings, very bright, Kurelek and his family are sitting in a field: a picnic with barns and yards in the background. Across the grass, little bits of paper scattering in the wind. He had begun the farm series, the humour and the joy; he had painted the dark stuff out.

I can remember him at his bench, see him working. There was about Kurelek the little boy, a studious, industrious little boy. The way his body would wrap around and protect his work: he worked close to himself, hunched over, leaning over his bench into his work. The look on his face: a slight compression of his lips and cheeks, a determined look, eyes tight, small, intense. The way his hands would move: small strokes, a small world going on.

Bill would break for coffee and cookies (both he and Stan loved coffee breaks and cookies). Bill always had a bag of cookies on his bench, and coffee makings. He'd work and have a coffee break. With the spoon in the mug, he'd crinkle up in pleasure. I can see him smiling, crumbling his cookie. The corners of his eyes would crinkle up and he would beam.

On Bill's bench there was a panel of a boy lying on the grass reading a book, a farm boy in blue jeans, red shirt, straw hat. Half finished, it was looking very like an impressionist painting. I said to Bill, "I like it. It's great." Bill looked at me, shocked. "It's not finished." Adamant. All the details would be put in, not just a red impression of a shirt, but a red checked shirt. You see the checks, the jeans have seams, the straw hat is tattered. This would all be drawn in, because THAT is the way it is.

Bill said to me many times he felt the twentieth century's gift to the artist was the camera.

Bill also had a dark humour. I saw, in the shop, a painting he was framing, which depicted a large cast-iron stove; to the left a number of little hands have just thrown the cat up onto the stove-top. The cat is arched and screeching. I was wide-eyed. "What's this about?" Bill said, "That's one of the jokes we'd play on the cat."

34

Eleven

In the *Fields* series of paintings there is one with a man standing in a field with outstretched arms. The wind is blowing patterns in the grasses. I asked Bill, "Who is that person?" He said that it was him. I told Bill it also reminded me of myself. He replied, "Yes, that too."

I had been invited to join the Kureleks' for dinner, encouraged to do so by his wife, Jean. Bill had very few male friends. Bill picked me up at the end of the day at the workshop and we drove off. I sat in the back seat; his eldest daughter in front. Driving down Sherbourne Street we slowed at a crosswalk. A bent-legged, hunchbacked man was standing at the corner. Bill stopped, leaned over and pointed for his daughter to see: "Look at the cripple," and drove on.

Bill pointed out the hand-carved plaque he'd painted of salt and bread, a traditional sign of Ukrainian welcome. We assembled in the front room, where Bill introduced his children. They were quiet, well-behaved and shy. Bill, proud to be teaching them Ukrainian, asked the children to exhibit their skill. They counted in Ukrainian and showed me their Ukrainian story books.

After grace, dinner became a family affair, with talk of school, jokes, and what the chldren wanted to be when they grew up.

Dinner finished, Jean took over washing up and putting the children to bed while Bill and I went down to his basement workroom. We talked about his art. He showed me books of Bosch and Breughel, explained how his vision was influenced by these artists, how he had learned to assemble his early allegorical pieces through studying these paintings. I could see the similarities, especially the depiction of man being small in the vastness of the world.

All through the evening Jean allowed us our visit by handling dinner and the children, animated yet quietly supportive. A lovely evening.

Bill dropped me off at the Main Street subway station. Leaning over to open my door, abruptly, almost impatiently, the close contact, for him, difficult.

Bill was also a father to me, especially when he taught me gilding. I came to work that morning; he was going to teach me; he did.

I had extreme difficulties with frame finishing at first. My hands were awkward, I didn't know the ins and outs of my materials, the tricks of the trade. The first frame I actually finished, all I could see were the flaws in it: horrible mistakes, ragged leaf breaks, how unprofessional it looked. I was convinced it looked like my ragged soul at that moment. This frame would be returned so fast — after all, it had been purchased for its look.

I had had a sample to follow. My frame was in no way close to this sample. Bill came over quietly and said, "It's all right. We all had to start." He actually gave me a hand with the frame. He had done the sample. He showed me how he stroked it, antiqued it. It was so quiet, so full; it was exactly what I needed. My inexperience was out in the open, absolutely visible, raw and painful. Bill was wonderful. It was a gift that he was there.

Laying imitation leaf on a frame with a particularly tight return (where two beadings meet) I was having difficulty with the leaf cracking and breaking, therefore exposing the red underlay. The sample showed no red. I was determined that I could do this and was heating up fast, pushing leaf into the return and trying to fix it. I couldn't do it. I would have to ask Bill for help. I found asking so hard. Bill came over quietly. By quietly I mean, no *whatsa matter, screwing up?*, none of that; he took a look at the situation and devised putting the imitation leaf on a piece of paper, sliding the paper across the frame, then releasing the gold at the edge of the paper so that I could protect it from breaking as it went down into the return. Bill took it seriously, actually said, "It's painful, isn't it?" Yes, it was.

Bill did teach me how to gild and finish. I learned the formulas he gave me. None of it was by measurement — no cups of this or teaspoons of that. Bill's children were all young at that time. They were going through huge quantities of apple juice and baby food. Bill brought juice tins and food jars from home. So instead of measuring things, it would be, almost up to the second line on the apple juice tin; or a full lid of clay or glue from a baby food jar. That's how I learned.

I became intrigued, fell in love with finishing. I started to read, tried to find as many books as I could on gilding. There are very few. I found some at the main reference library; not able to take them out, I copied down formulas. One of the most valuable for a good gilding job was a pyramid of glue strengths: the strength lessening in proportion as you reached the pinnacle of the finish, the actual gold. This would prevent cracking at the burnishing stage.

At this time two things occurred: through practise and reading my gilding was more proficient, and the workshop had a frame to do for the retiring Lieutenant Governor of Ontario, Charlie Comfort's portrait of Ross MacDonald for Queen's Park. It was my chance, my master's piece. It was up to me to put all my knowledge into this one frame. No expense was spared; I laid three layers of gold leaf. When the frame was burnished, totally burnished, the solidity of the gold lit up the finishing end of the shop in gold light.

Just prior to finishing this frame, realizing that we had the job and I would be doing it, I spoke to Bill about the pyramid of glue strengths, showing him what I had learned. Bill turned to me and said, "Now you're on your own. You know more than me." I was the student who'd graduated. He wasn't the teacher pulling me back; he let me go.

Bill not only taught me gilding; Bill, Stan and the workshop taught me a tradition. Raw mouldings shoved into a machine and pooped out the other end with computerized antiquing are dead. The product of skill and craft from the painter is only served by the frame that wraps around an artwork, by the skill and craft of the framer. The hand-work taught me. The accident that could be used rather than tripped over was not only a skill I could market into my own business, but a skill that could surround and live with some of the greatest art this world had ever produced. Not only the Canadian scene that could revere Tom Thomson or Milne, but the world of the Impressionists, the Old Masters, because the leap to the spiritual was through a manipulation of the organic. The gesso rubbed, the clay painted, the gold burnished: he gave it to me. Quietly, quietly, he gave it to me.

A Kurelek "Classic" Frame

One of the finest examples of Kurelek's classic work, a reproduction of a Spanish/Italian frame, is set up in threes. The lip and cap are gilded with silver leaf, as is the panel. The panel, however, is painted over in black; a design is then scratched through the paint, revealing the silver underneath. The sides are painted a dull red.

Tale of a Dog

On my bench one morning was a painting one inch wide and thirteen inches tall, a gift from Bill. It was entitled "Tale of a Dog." The painting depicts a stand of trees in the background, a post in the middle ground, and in the foreground, walking off to the left, the hindquarters of a dog with a large tail. It is a snow scene. The painting has three levels of meaning and humour: the TAIL of the dog — we actually see it; the TALE of the dog as he wanders from the stand of trees, his footprints in the snow, to the post in the middle ground where the dog has done its duty; there's also the reason the painting is one inch wide and thirteen inches tall — the painting itself is the tale of a dog job, a dog job being any job that didn't go well. In this case, Bill had mis-measured the painting, made a frame only to find the painting one inch too large. Practical as ever, he sawed the one inch off.

39

Twelve

THE TOOL PAINTINGS

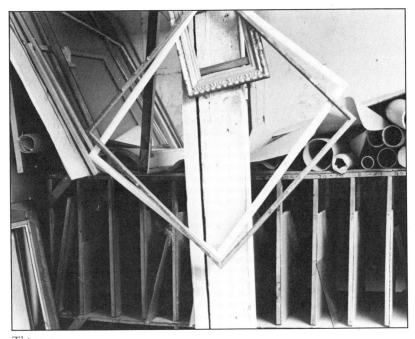

Thirteen

Framer's Wire

There is an intimacy to this piece, a very close look at something used in a day of work but unregarded, an intimacy created by its particularity, its focused view. The roll is given focus by its central location within the picture. The eye is led to the roll by the pliers, the startling red pliers pointing towards centre from the bottom right. The eye is not allowed to wander off by the limitation of the background stretching across the picture behind the roll, the black edge of a picture frame. The wire roll, trapped by these pictorial elements, becomes located. Intimacy is derived from a sense of completion. The frame in the background has been wired, the last job before the frame is sent out. The sense of rest is the visually set quality of the "scene:" the frame wired, the actual roll of wire, pliers laid to rest. The job done, quietly complete.

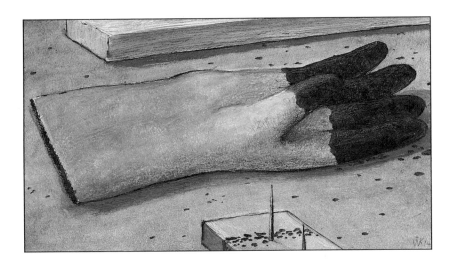

Frame Finisher's Glove

This painting, for me, is ominous. The upright nails are sharpened concrete nails driven through a piece of pine 1 X 2", onto which a frame is pressed. The glove is used to protect the hand from the aniline stain which is spread around the frame. Here, however, Kurelek has caught the glove as a hand. The sharp nails and the drips of stain convey the ominous. If the hand slips, it is gashed. I cringe over this picture because I have gashed myself in this way. Yet after that initial shock, there is another feeling present, deeper; the glove is such a human thing, and I find it here abandoned, lost, quietly wrenching. The glove becomes a trace, the memory of a working hand.

The first pictorial exploration of Bill Kurelek's interest in framing was shown in the O *Toronto* exhibition: a drawing of the workshop for which the photographs included here were the basis. In the O *Toronto* book, Kurelek speaks about the workshop:

Before I became a full-time painter, I was a finisher, and worked a good deal gilding frames with silver and gold. I still make my own frames there, for I really love the work. It's physically satisfying and also quite creative to be able to plan one's own frames. In his book The Natural Way to Draw, *Kimon Nikolaides stresses that a tradesman could probably do a more meaningful drawing of the materials or tools of his trade than an outsider such as an artist. This is because he knows them in a tactile experiential way.*

After the exhibition of the Workshop drawing in O *Toronto*, it seems Kurelek took the quote he'd borrowed from Kimon Nikolaides about the drawing of tools to heart, and began painting them. The first ones shown here were laid out on Bill's work bench one morning. Having missed the late night bus to his farm near Combermere, Bill decided to come to the shop, not to sleep, but to paint.

In all these and the tool paintings there is a common visual thread. Kurelek, known for his large landscapes, the wide prairie view, reveals another side of his work. Not that it wasn't there before, just overshadowed by the vast space of his other, better known work. The larger, publicly acclaimed pieces, especially those paintings or shows receiving reviews, were addressed solely on content, at the expense of an analysis of how Kurelek made art.

The elements of composition and architecture, Kurelek's draftsmanship, become clear in the tool paintings. These paintings are simple; their directness shows Kurelek's eye for details, his regard for small common things, seen by their elevation into painting as something new, something larger. These paintings catch particular tools as to take them out of their context, in such a way that they can no longer be taken for granted as daily tools. They are so large within the picture plane they demand recognition, demand that you see them beyond their utility.

The tool paintings also exhibit crossover techniques from picture framing. Kurelek employs smudge and spatter techniques used in framing for antiquing to lend both texture and shade to the portrayed objects.

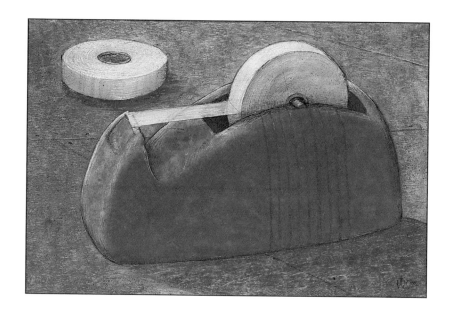

Tape Dispenser

From all the tools to choose from, this one has to be the most pedestrian. Yet after spending time with the painting, it conveys its utilitarian lumpishness, conveys successfully the weight that is necessary to its function. It sits proudly, if not a little ponderously, before us, in all its glorious proletarian green. The mere painting of this object raises it from its ignobility and gives it stature. This is Kurelek's humour. I am reminded of a print that Kurelek made showing a large pig sticking its snout through a slatted fence, the title being, "I'm Beautiful." This is the same piece.

The Blacking Brush

Used only for blacking, this brush had been around long before I worked at the shop. It was long, thick, and totally ink-encrusted. It worked perfectly. In the painting it looms large beside the squeezed tubes and the fat gum eraser in the foreground. The very size of the painting allows the length of the brush to assume its true proportions. I can remember thinking when I first held it, that it was unlike any brush I had ever seen. It was huge, with all the characteristics of a normal size brush. The power of the painting is such that I can feel it in my hand. I believe anybody can.

Fourteen

CHANGES

Bill's ten years are up. His paintings are selling. He comes to the shop only to frame his work.

A succession of finishers finish according to his samples. Gus, Dennis, Rasheid, myself.

Bill moves out. Stan stays.

Av, busy in the gallery as it begins to sail on its own, becomes the master of two ships.

A number of fitters come and go, some slow, others always late; one who dumps the change from his pay envelope and saves only the bills.

Bill the night owl works graveyard so as not to interfere in the daily work.

Fifteen

Cutting up barnboard for frames, Bill doesn't remove the nails, which dull and wreck the saw blades.

Stan complains about the blades.

Bill buys his own blades.

The cost of glass, matboard and moulding continues to rise.

As Bill's reputation grows, he travels and is gone for longer lengths of time.

Moulding now has to be bought in five hundred foot lots. Before, it was bought as needed in bundles of fifty or a hundred feet.

Bill buys a farm in Combermere and spends time there.

Sixteen

The compressor for spraying lacquer is cantankerous. I spend more and more time fixing it. I ask Stan to look at it. He agrees with me that it ought to be replaced. I ask Av in to take a look. Av asks Stan what he thinks. Stan says everything is fine.

Stan talks about owning a cottage up north at coffee breaks.

Av asks Stan for a set of shelves to go along the north wall of the office. Stan asks how high.

Bill, busier than ever, hires helpers for his frame work.

An article on Bill finds its way into the shop. He is noted as a master framer. Stan scoffs.

Stan's son gets married and Stan feels he has no more responsibilities.

Seventeen

Stan and I have an argument over the coffee cream I have used and didn't replace. This flares up while working at my bench. Stan paces back and forth behind me and I feel I am being watched. We ask Av into the shop to mediate. I see quite clearly Stan misses Av's presence in the shop and say so. Av admits that he is weighed down with administrative duties. Stan, with difficulty, explains how he feels the shop has been abandoned. Av speaks of his fondness for the shop, but realizes he no longer knows what goes on daily. He also misses Bill.

Stan gets arthritis in his hands and cannot press the stapler to stretch a canvas.

Av mentions to Stan that rent for the shop has almost doubled. Stan is convinced Av will close the shop.

Stan goes into the gallery and quarrels with Av. After eleven years, Stan gives one week's notice.

Av is shaken.

Eighteen

We give a party for Stan, and present him with a gift: an oak and silver cookie jar stuffed with his favourite cookies.

Now that Stan has gone, Av no longer feels obliged to keep the shop open.

Av asks if I'll stay. I set up a small shop in the basement of the gallery.

When I tell Av I'm leaving to set up my own business he is angry, angry and speechless.

Av sells me moulding and equipment dirt cheap. He refers his framing customers to me.

I go back to the shop every now and then. Remembering. Dust and benches, a broken chair, lengths of moulding. Remembering bits and pieces of daily work, crumpled sandpaper, a stick of graphite next to a red stain on a bench top, the smell of shellac and cut walnut, the sound of a saw whining down a length of wood, frames made for the Parliament Buildings in Ottawa, for Picassos, Tom Thomsons, Milnes and Averys. I remember voices with the satisfaction of something well done or the grunt of it going badly. Bill. Stan. Av.

The walls are bare and the rooms are empty except for the dust. Three rooms. One for each of us: the finisher, the cutter, the fitter. We called the fitting room "the fitting end." Kurelek, a lover of puns, painted a large black raven over the entrance and gave it a balloon: NEVERMORE. The rooms are bare, and crowded with the raven.

INDEX OF PHOTOGRAPHS, DRAWINGS
AND COLOUR PLATES

Photographs:

Page 40
12. Detail of cutting room with Stan Beecham replacing fuses, a frequent occurrence.
Page 41
13. Detail of glass storage bunk in fitting room.
Page 48
14. Detail of art storage bunk in fitting room.
Page 50
15. View of basement and hardwood storage bunks. Note Kurelek's supply of barnboards standing against back wall.
Page 52
16. View of basement showing softwood storage.
Page 54
17. Detail of moulding storage bunks in cutting room.
Page 56
18. View of finishing room through to back doors. On the left is the spray booth and to the right the finishing rack where lengths of moulding were prepared. At back left are crates spewing shredded newspaper for shipping Eskimo sculpture.

These photographs, with the exception of No. 6, were taken by William Kurelek in 1971.

Frame (Colour Plate):

Page 38
A Kurelek "Classic" Frame

Paintings (Colour Plates):

Page 39
"Tale of a Dog" Mixed media on masonite, 1975
13" X 1"

Page 42
"Framer's Wire" Mixed media on masonite, 1974
7 3/8" X 12 3/8"

Cover; page 43
"Frame Finisher's Glove" Mixed media on masonite, 1974
6 7/8" X 12 3/8"

Page 46
"Tape Dispenser" Mixed media on masonite, 1974
8 1/2" X 12 1/4"

Page 47
"The Blacking Brush" Mixed media on masonite, 1974
3 3/4" X 15"

Drawings:

Page 22
"Work Order" Pencil drawing on card, 1970
13 1/4" X 7 5/8"
From the collection of Marlene and Robert Markle

Page 31
"When the Boss Is Away" Pencil and collage on paper, 1965
12" X 15 3/4"
with Isaacs frame label

Page 59
"The Isaacs Gallery Workshop" Mixed media drawing, 1971
30" X 22"

Brian Dedora was born in Vernon, B.C., in 1946, and received a B.A. from the University of Victoria in 1970. He is a writer and performance artist whose work has been anthologized and widely published in special and limited editions. He is the author of *White Light*. This is his second major book publication.

Other fine books from Aya Press/The Mercury Press:

Vivid: Stories by Five Women
Figures in Paper Time: Fictions *Richard Truhlar*
1988: Selected Poems & Texts *Gerry Shikatani*
Love & Hunger: An Anthology of New Fiction
The Blue House *Lesley McAllister*
Ink and Strawberries: An Anthology of
      Quebec Women's Fiction
Hundred Proof Earth *Milton Acorn*
In England Now That Spring *bpNichol & Steve McCaffery*
Arcana for a Silent Voice *Peter Baltensperger*
Empty Sky Go on Unending *Marjory Smart*
White Light *Brian Dedora*

Please write for our complete catalogue:

Aya Press/The Mercury Press
Box 446
Stratford, Ontario
Canada N5A 6T3